Andrey Tikhomirov

# The Chronicle of Russia and the USSR (from ancient times to 1960)

**Andrey Tikhomirov**

# The Chronicle of Russia and the USSR (from ancient times to 1960)

## Brief description of history and culture

**ScienciaScripts**

# Table of contents

# Introduction

"The chronicle has not ceased to be a leading genre of Russian literature."

Dmitry LIKHACHEV (1906-1999),

academician, philologist, historian of Old Russian literature, public figure

"The chronicle    is the most important historical source that has no equal."

Mikhail Nikolaevich Tikhomirov (1893-1965),

academician, historian, head of the group for publishing the complete collection of Russian annals

"Russian annals are ahead of events and testify to all-Russian interests, to the unity of the Russian land."

Alexei Shakhmatov (1864-1920),

academician, linguist, historian of Russian literature, researcher of Russian chronicles

*Nestor the Chronicler. Bronze. Sculptor M.M. Antokolsky. 1890 г.*

History is the memory of all humanity, the foundation of its activities and culture. The whole way of mankind goes through the prism of historical knowledge, making us think, learn and understand a lot. Nothing arises from an empty place. All the achievements of modern times are based on the lessons of the past. Textbooks and learning aids play a huge role in the study of history, but they do provide the idea of history through the interpretation of the author. Meanwhile, in order to study history in a versatile and unbiased way, it is necessary to rely on primary sources, to get directly acquainted with real events.

The presented historical material can be used in any educational audience, for writing reports and abstracts, allows to expand considerably the outlook on history.

You can keep thousands of facts in your memory and not know the history, not be able to understand it. With the help of the "Chronicle" you can create your own works on the basis of the received data, write scientific works, build your own versions and interpretations of the development of Russia. Behind dry facts it is necessary to see mutual relations of events and the phenomena, live, real images of people, their struggle, defeats and victories.

The purpose of the Annals is to help to slightly expand the scope of textbooks based on

of what was officially published in the press pages at the time. It is important to find the facts needed for a certain topic in the "Chronicles" and to bring them to your works so that they have a convincing appearance and could confirm the conclusions of the author. The facts given in the Annals are not a certain selection of data, but express the general trend of the time to which they relate.

Chronicles - the most important political documents of Russian existence - were and are the most visible and significant manifestation of past and present life. Consistently and continuously recording events, the chronicles seem to bring them together, creating a vast panorama of state existence, without which nothing could be understood in Russian history. Imagine for a second that we do not have chronicles - and a huge muddy grey spot would be on the place of a complex, bright and dynamic Russian life, full of political, ideological, cultural, economic and social events!

The undisputed historical facts from the chronicles were and are referred to by the unification of the Russian lands, inextricably linking the times with this state policy, reviving and shaping the national consciousness of the Russian people. The annals persistently emphasized continuity of authority, its political and economic continuity during all period of chronicle writing, and it is known since XI century though there are separate data also about earlier origin of chronicle writing in Russia.

Academician D.S. Likhachev called Russian chronicle a grandiose phenomenon of Russian culture. Under current conditions, chronicle writing needs support from all progressive and advanced forces to serve as a source of knowledge and literary inspiration for all people.

# Celebrating New Year in Russia

The main attributes of any year alternate day and night, returning them back to their original positions. That is we are talking about winter and summer solstices, spring and autumn equinoxes. These moments of the year were celebrated by the ancient Eastern Slavs (ancestors of Russians, Ukrainians and Byelorussians) as a certain beginning.

The oldest system of counting time for East Slavic tribes, whose farms were based on agricultural production, was most likely counting the seasons: spring, summer, autumn, winter. The full period of change of seasons was called "summer". Weather records of the Russian annals began with the words "in summer", which means "a year". Many ritual pagan festivals were connected with the agricultural calendar, with the seasons of the year, which later became Christian. These are, for example, Shrovetide, carol (from the Latin "calendar"; another name of this holiday "oatmeal" - from "o-spring", Oatmeal - New Year, the word may have come from the word "oatmeal", "oatmeal", an agricultural crop usually placed in crop rotations after grain winter crops of legumes, flax. Oat grain in whole form is used mainly for feeding horses, and horses are sacred beings of ancient Slavs. Like other peoples, the Slavs deified the phenomena of nature, animals, plants, some human properties (knowledge, skills), because they could not give explanations for their growth, changes, actions, etc., here are, for example, some names of Russian folk songs: "Call of spring", "Berezonka", "Garden", "Sowing flax", "Invitation to the street", "Ovsen", "Wonderful pike", "White swan and grey geese", "Horse", "Born", "Ivushka", "Ryabinushka", "Falcon in a cage", etc.), which marked the turn of the sun in summer, "red slide" - the feast of the meeting of spring, "rainbow" and "mermaid" - spring and summer memorial festivals and others. Kolyada is a pre-Christian cycle of festivals among the Slavs during the winter solstice. According to ancient views, it is the beginning of a new life, the renewal of nature, and thus the beginning of the new year. Carols are accompanied by carols (songs and rituals). In the content of carols and their analogue in Ukraine and Belarus - generous - researchers identify more than 80 motives, the main are: goodwill, glorification and spell. After the introduction of Christianity, the church included it in its Christmas and baptismal cycles from December 24 to January 19 (the time of saints - that is, the increase in daylight). The church opposed "glorification of Christ", walking with a star, and other Christian attributes to the games and rites of the carols. As a result there was a syncretic (mixed) ritual.

The inseparable connection with nature is shown by the Old Russian names of months: January was called shingles (the light part of the day increased noticeably, it became lighter), February - lectern (this name reflected the occupation of slash-and-burn agriculture, it was the time of felling the forest), March - dry (felled trees dried up, and in some places the ground), April - birch or birch ash (the beginning of birch blossoming in southern regions, the transformation of burnt trees into ash), May - grass (time of grass appearance), June - isok (grasshopper), July - worm or sickle (time of reaping), August - dawn (from "dawn" - probably, the beginning of deer roar during the autumn gonna), September - rueen (from the verb "rueit" - roar) or herring (most likely from heathei, juniper, blooming in autumn), October - foliage, November and December were called breasts ("pile" - frozen road track), less often - jelly.

Together with Christianity in Russia the Julian calendar and the Roman names of the months, fixed in one of the most ancient monuments of Russian writing - the Ostromian Gospel have extended. Many ancient Russian names of months were preserved in Ukrainian and Byelorussian languages.

In Ancient Russia was known to count time in weeks, seven days each. From here comes the Old Russian name of the week "week". Unlike many ancient calendars, in which the days of the week were called by the names of the planets dedicated to the ancient gods - Mars, Mercury, Jupiter, Venus, Saturn, the ancient Russian names of days reflected their orderly position relative to the Sunday, called "week" (from "not to do" - not to work, as it was a day of rest). The next day was Monday (after the week), then

- Tuesday (second after the week), Wednesday (middle of the week), Thursday (fourth), Friday (fifth day after the "week"). Saturday (in Slavic "six" or "six") got its name from the Hebrew word "sabbath" (shabbat), which meant rest. The same day of the week is associated with the modern Russian expression "six" in the meaning of "incorrect", "uncertain", "two-faced", as the Slavic name of the day of the week has not survived, and was, in fact, forcibly used by us the famous word "sabbath". Sunday (Resurrection) - a weekly Christian holiday, established in honor of the Resurrection of Jesus Christ, became in Russia the name of the day of the week.

The seven-day week dates back to the Chaldean-Babylonian astronomical calculations, and was borrowed by the ancient Jews, who celebrated the end of the divine creation of the world as a feast day. The Sabbath was also celebrated in original Christianity, disassociating Christians from Judaism and celebrating as a holiday the first day of the week on which Christ's resurrection took place.

The surviving names of the days of the week associated with astral cults have survived in some European countries to this day, for example: German Montag, English Monday - day of the moon (Monday), Sonntag, Sunday - day of the sun (Sunday), French Vendredi - day of Venus (Friday), English Vendredi - day of Venus (Friday).

- Saturday is Saturn's day (Saturday) and other words.

It is not known exactly what day the week began and ended in Ancient Russia. It is believed that in everyday life the beginning of the week was Sunday and the end was Saturday, but in church practice the week usually began on Monday and ended on Sunday.

After the adoption of Christianity in 988-989 the calendar "from the creation of the world" was introduced (on the Byzantine model), the New Year was celebrated from March 1. Under Ivan III from 1492. (7000 "from the creation of the world"), the New Year began to be celebrated from September 1. Peter I in 1700 introduced a new (Julian) calendar "from the Nativity of Christ", New Year was celebrated from January 1. Under the Soviet rule in 1918 was introduced the current Gregorian calendar, which now goes ahead of the Julian calendar for 13 days, so Russia also celebrates the old New Year.

The modern international era is the era from the Nativity of Christ (in literature it is denoted: before R. X., after R. X., before or after our, or new era). It was created in 525 by a Roman monk, the papal archivist Dionysius the Little, a Scythian by birth. When compiling Easter, Dionysius calculated the year of Christ's birth - 754 from the foundation of Rome or 284 BC to the beginning of the Diocletian era. In the VI century this era spread in Western Europe, and by the XIX century in all Christian countries. In Russia it has been entered by Peter I since January 1, 1700.

# The sketch of Russian history

The ancestors of the Slavs have long lived in Central and Eastern Europe. In the language they concern to Indo-European peoples which inhabit Europe and a part of Asia down to India. Archaeologists believe that Slavic tribes can be traced on the data of excavations from the middle of the second millennium BC. Ancestors of Slavs (in the scientific literature they name Praslavs) presumably find among the tribes inhabiting pool of the Odra, Vistula and Dnepr; in pool of Danube and on Balkans Slavic tribes have appeared only in the beginning of AD.

The estimated maximum settlement area of the Slavic ancestors in the west reached the Elbe (Laba), in the north to the Baltic Sea, in the east - to the Seimas and Oka, and in the south their border was a wide strip of forest-steppe, going from the left bank of the Danube to the east in the direction of Kharkov. This territory was inhabited by several hundred Slavic tribes.

In VI century from uniform Slavic community the East Slavic branch (the future Russian, Ukrainian, Byelorussian people) is allocated. Approximately by this time occurrence of the large tribal unions of east Slavs concerns. The chronicle has kept a legend about reigning in Middle Dnicpcr of brothers Kija, Schek, Horiv and their sisters Lybedi and about the basis of Kiev. The same reigning was in other tribal unions, including 100-200 separate tribes.

The realm of settlement of the Proto-Slavs which, as linguists believe, have separated from the Balts related to them in the middle of 1 thousand BC, was rather small. In early sources Praslavs were called Venetians and communicated both with Germanic tribes, and with Finns (not modern Finns). From here it is possible to make an assumption that Venedas occupied approximately territory of present southeast Poland, Southwest Byelorussia and Northwest Ukraine. During the 2nd century the Slavs pushed back or assimilated some other peoples from the Baltic Sea coast and, later, occupied the areas of the Carpathians.

The Hun invasion led to significant population movements. Approximately at the same time as the Turks settled in the steppe part of South-East Europe, its forest-steppe part was gradually mastered by the Slavs, who by the 5th century had already reached the Middle Dnieper. Then they advanced to the basin of the river Desna, which received the Slavic name (Right). Interestingly, the main part of the large rivers in the south preserved their old, Iranian names. Thus, the Don is just a river, the Dnieper is explained as a deep river, the Ros is a light river, the Prut is a river, etc.

Till 6 century the Byzantium historiographers hardly mention Slavs, but later the information on them starts to grow. It is connected, most likely, with the beginning of active colonization of the Balkans by Slavs (they have come close to the Byzantium borders). Byzantines divided Slavs into two groups. The western Slavs were called as Slavs (folds, warehouses). The Balkan Slavs also concerned to them. But, besides, mentioned Anta which were considered special, most likely east, group of Slavs.

The Byzantine writers singled out the antes as the bravest of the Slavs. It is curious, that antes and folds often enmity with each other and it was skillfully used by Byzantines, even more colliding the northern neighbors.

The main occupation of the Eastern Slavs was farming. This is confirmed by archaeological excavations where seeds of cereals (rye, barley, millet) and vegetable crops (turnip, cabbage, carrots, beet, radish) were found. Technical crops (flax, hemp) were also grown.

The big role in economy of east Slavs as in all societies at a stage of decay of a tribal system, military extraction played: tribal leaders made raids to Byzantium, extracting there slaves and luxury goods.

Around the 7th - 8th centuries the craft was finally separated from farming. The ancient Slavs were pagans who deified the forces of nature. The main god was probably Rod, the god of heaven and earth. He was surrounded by the female deities of fertility - Rozhanitsa. An important role was also played by deities associated with the forces of nature, which are especially important for agriculture: Yarilo - god of the sun (in some Slavic tribes he was called Yarilo, Khoros) and Perun - god of thunder and lightning.

Also known are the "cattle god" Volos, or Beleye, Dazhdbog, Stribog, Samargla, Svarog (god of fire) Mokosha (goddess of earth and fertility), etc. The gods were offered sacrifices, sometimes even human ones. The pagan cult was set out in specially arranged temples, where the idol was placed. Formation of the state at east Slavs was a natural result of long process of decomposition of a tribal system and transition to a class society. The process of property and social stratification among community members led to the separation of the most affluent part from their environment. The tribal and wealthy part of the community, subordinating the mass of ordinary community members, needs to maintain its domination in state structures.

According to the Story of time years, the Russian princely dynasty originates in Novgorod. Modern science, using the Nestor's Chronicle, multi-lingual early medieval sources and rich archaeological material, has no doubt that at the end of V - beginning of VI centuries on the middle Dnieper was formed the Kiev state - Princedom of Glades. Prince Kiy also put Kievitets, a town on the Danube, sailed to Constantinople. And in the north approximately at the same time another princedom was created, where, according to Joachim's annals, the first prince was someone Slaven, then his three sons - Izbor, Vladimir and Stolposvet reigned, and the descendant of Vladimir the Ancient in the ninth generation of Buriva was the father of Novgorod prince Gostomysl, on which this dynasty was interrupted. "This Gostomysl is a brave and wise husband, all his neighbors are terrible, and people are loved, the massacre for justice. This for the sake of the aperture I read him and his gifts and gifts to give, buying the world from him. Many princes from the distant countries to the parishioner by sea and land to listen to the wisdom, and see the judgment of his, and ask for advice and teachings of his, as those famous everywhere. It is remarkable, that, unlike the Kiev history where between Kiem and his descendants Askold and Dir - dark failure in some centuries, Novgorodians have kept in memory not only some Dorurikov's names of princes, but also some details of antiquity.

Gostomysl had four sons, all of whom died in the wars, and three "daughters were given out as wives by the seventh prince". And so Gostomysl on the slope of the years is left without an heir and one day allegedly dreams, as if "from the womb of the middle daughters of his Umila" grows a wonderful tree - "from his fruit is saturated people of all the earth. Has Gostomysl actually had such a dream, or has he simply chosen a worthy heir for his reason? "The people of Gostomysl decide: "From her sons she shall inherit him, and the earth shall be satisfied with his reigning".

Soon Gostomysl, "seeing the end of his stomach, calling all the oldest of the Slavs (Slovenes), Rus, Chudis, Vesi, Meri, Krivich and Trevich, showed them a dream and the ambassador of the chosen in the Varangians to ask the prince.

Thus, according to "The Agenda of time years" the representative of a tribe Russ with family and team has been invited for board in already existing Slavic state. The way of a calling of prince with a team has been widely distributed in Europe in the early Middle Ages. In itself the calling of foreign prince did not change the Slavic nature of an existing society. However to speak about pure Slavic sources of Russian ethnos would be a big stretch. The Old Russian nation was formed on the basis of wide interaction of several subethnic components. It is formed as an ethnic community on the basis of connection of three economic and technological regions of agricultural, cattle breeding and trade, and, consequently, three ways of life - sedentary, nomadic, vagrant, in a mixture of several ethnic streams: Slavic, Baltic, with a notable influence of the Turkic.

The state of Eastern Slavs was formed in IX-X centuries. Its territorial nucleus was the union of fields with the center in Kiev (which received not later than the beginning of IX century. political and geographical name "Rus"). In IX-X centuries there is a submission of authority of the Kiev princes of other East Slavic unions of tribal princedoms. By the end of X century this process comes to an end and a structure of the uniform state consisting of large territorial units - the volosts operated by Princes - governors of the Kiev prince develops.

In Kievan Rus, as in other states of early feudal Europe, a feudal society is formed. The formation of feudal relations in Russia was generally of the pan-European type: from state forms to senorial (patrimonial). But unlike Western Europe, where the traditions of private property of antiquity caused the rapid growth of senorial landownership, in Russia this process was much slower.

In IX century is formed system of operation personally free population by military service nobility ("team") of the Kiev princes by collecting a tribute - "poodja", in X century, there is a domain (patrimonial) land tenure of the Kiev princes. In XI century land property appears at representatives of the top of served nobility - boyars and Christian church. In XII - first half of XIII centuries patrimonial land ownership grows, but even during this period its role in comparison with state-feudal forms remains secondary. Most producers continue to be land dependent only on the state power represented by the princes and their vigilantes, and are exploited by the collection of tribute and other state taxes.

In the middle of XII century Russia enters the period of feudal fragmentation (Western Europe accordingly - in X - XII centuries). The single state, consisting of and" volosts, is divided into a number of independent principalities - the lands: Kiev, Chernigov, Smolensk, Volyn, Galicia, Vladimir-Suedal, Novgorod, Polotsk, Pereyaslavl, Murom, Ryazan, Turovo-Pinsk. The majority of them has fastened to certain branches of the expanded Old Russian Princely sort Rurikovich. Borders of the grounds did not coincide neither with pre-state borders of the unions of tribal princedoms, nor with the later division into three now existing East Slavic peoples (Russians, Ukrainians, Byelorussians). The social and economic precondition for the isolation of the principalities was the development and complication of the system of state feudalism, as well as the formation of princely domains, "fixing" the separate branches of the princely family to certain territories. Lands, each of which was the size of a large European state, became independent subjects of international relations.

The formation of the Old Russian spiritual culture was notable for its significant peculiarity. It was formed as a result of synthesis of the Slavic pagan culture with the culture, access to which was opened by Russia with the adoption at the end of X century. 8 as a state religion of the Eastern (Byzantine) version of Christianity. An important factor was the perception of this culture through writing in the Slavic language understood by the population. (Created by Cyril and Methodius in the second half of IX century the Slavic writing has received development in the Slavic states which have professed Christianity in east variant - in Russia, in Bulgaria and Serbia). Unlike the countries of Western Europe, and also the Slavic states (Poland and Czechia) in which the western Catholic variant of Christianity has confirmed and where language of divine service (from here - and the literature) was Latin, in Russia, and also in Bulgaria and Serbia church service was made in Slavic language and the literature was Slavic speaking. In many respects thanks to it after acceptance of Christianity to Russia the considerable quantity of the Slavic-language literature, mainly church has arrived (basically and" Bulgaria, becoming the Christian country on century earlier). Through it (and partly through Greek books, which arrived in Russia and were translated here) Russia became acquainted with the cult" frames: ancient, Middle Eastern, early Christian, Byzantine, Slavic Christian. Already in the XI century there appeared original Russian literature, which by its achievements became the most significant branch of Russian medieval culture.

Three most influential states have been formed on the territory of Kievan Rus: the Vladimir-Suzdal Principality (North-Eastern Russia), the Galicia-Volyn Principality (South-Western Russia) and the Novgorod Land (North-Western Russia). Both within these principalities, and between them, for a long time^ were fierce collisions, destructive wars, which weakened the force of Russia, led to the destruction of cities and villages.

The foreign conquerors did not fail to take advantage of this circumstance. Uncoordinated actions of Russian princes, the desire to achieve victory over the enemy at the expense of others, while maintaining its army, the lack of a unified command led to the first defeat of the Russian army in the battle with the Tatar-

Mongols on the river Kalka May 31, 1223 Serious disagreements between the princes, which did not allow them to act as a united front in the face of Tatar-Mongolian aggression led to the capture and destruction of Ryazan (1237). In February 1238 the Russian militia on the river Sit was defeated, Vladimir and Suzdal were captured. In October 1239 it was besieged and Chernigov was captured, in autumn 1240 Kiev was captured. Thus, from the beginning of the 40s of the XIII century begins the period of Russian history, which is commonly called the Tatar-Mongol yoke, which lasted until the second half of the XV century.

It should be noted that the Tatar-Mongols did not occupy Russian lands during this period, as this territory was of little use for economic and economic activities of nomadic peoples. But this yoke was very real. Russia found itself in vassal dependence on Tatar-Mongol khans. Each prince, including the Grand Duke, had to get the permission of the khan to rule - "table", khan's label. The population of the Russian lands has been enclosed by a heavy tribute in favor of Mongols, constantly made raids of conquerors which led to ruin of the lands and destruction of the population.

At the same time in the north-western borders of Russia there appeared a new dangerous enemy - in 1240 the Swedes, and then in 1240-1242 German crusaders. It turned out that the Novgorod land had to defend its independence and its type of development, under pressure from both East and West. The struggle for independence of the Novgorod land was led by the young prince Alexander Yaroslavich. His tactics were based on the struggle against the Catholic West and the concession to the East (Golden Horde). As a result the Swedish armies which have landed in July, 1240 in a mouth of Neva have been broken by a group of the Novgorod prince who has received for this victory honorable nickname "Nevsky".

Following the Swedes, the Novgorod land was attacked by German knights who settled in the Baltics at the beginning of XIII century. In 1240 they captured Izborsk, then Pskov. Alexander Nevskiy, who led the struggle against crusaders, managed to liberate Pskov first in winter 1242, and then on the ice of Chudskoye lake in the famous ice battle (April 5, 1242) to make a decisive defeat to German knights. After that they made no serious attempts to seize Russian lands.

Thanks to the efforts of Alexander Nevskiy and his descendants in the Novgorod land, in spite of dependence on the Golden Horde, the traditions of western orientation were preserved and the features of podtsanichestvo began to form.

However as a whole by the end of XIII century Northeast and Southern Russia have got under influence of Golden Horde, have lost communications with the West and earlier formed features of progressive development. It is difficult to overestimate those negative consequences which the Tatar-Mongol yoke had for Russia. The majority of historians agree in opinion, that the Tatar-Mongol yoke has essentially detained social and economic, political and spiritual development of the Russian state, has changed character of statehood, having given it the form of the relations characteristic for nomadic peoples of Asia.

It is known that in the fight against the Tatar-Mongols the first blow was taken by the princely squads. The overwhelming majority of them died. Together with the old nobility, the traditions of vassal and friendly relations went away. Now, as the new nobility formed, the relationship of subordination was established. Relations between princes and cities have changed. Veche (except for Novgorod land) lost its meaning. The prince in such conditions acted as the only protector and master.

Thus, the Russian statehood begins to acquire the features of Eastern despotism with its cruelty, arbitrariness, complete disregard for the people and personality. As a result, Russia has formed a kind of feudalism, which is quite strongly represented "Asian element". Formation of such original type of feudalism was promoted by that as a result of Tatar-Mongolian yoke Russia 240 years developed in isolation from Europe.

Russian Princedoms did not enter directly into the territory of the Golden Horde: dependence was expressed in payment of taxes (among which the main place was occupied by a per capita tribute - "exit") and the supreme suzerainty of the Golden Horde Khan who asserted Russian princes on tables. The question about the extent of the influence of the Mongol-Tatar invasion and the yoke on the Russian history has long been one of the discussion groups. First, they are those who recognize the very significant and mostly positive influence of the conquerors on the development of Russia, which manifested itself in the creation (thanks to them) of a single Russian (Moscow) state. The founder of this view was N. M. Karamzin.

Other historians (among them S. M. Solovyov, V. O. Klyuchevsky) estimated the impact of the conquerors on the internal life of the Old Russian society as extremely insignificant.

Finally, many researchers are characterized by a kind of "intermediate" position, in which the influence of the conquerors is considered as noticeable, extremely negative, but not determining for the development of the country. Such a point of view prevails in the Soviet historiography of Drabova V. D. Grekov, A. N. Nasokoz, V. V. Kargalova, etc.).

The volume of knowledge about economic, social, political, cultural development of Russian lands of XIII-XV centuries, about Russian-Horde relations allows to give the following estimation of influence of conquerors on various parties of Old Russian civilization.

The direct impact on the economy was expressed in the devastation of territories during the Horde's campaigns, and before all cities. In addition, the conquest led to the systematic pumping of significant material resources out of the country.

As a result of the invasion, the southern and western Russian lands were weakened in the XIV - early XV centuries, they were included in the Grand Duchy of Lithuania and partly in the Kingdom of Poland. Russian statehood (under the suzerainty of the Horde) remained in the North-Eastern (Vladimir-Suzdal) Russia and Novgorod land. As a result, a single Old Russian nation ceased to exist in the territories of North-Eastern and North-Western Russia, the Russian (Veliky Novgorod) nation began to form, and on the lands that became part of Lithuania and Poland - the Ukrainian and Belarusian people.

As a result of the invasion, the development of feudalism is slowing down, including the process of forming patrimonial land property. There is the conservation of state forms of exploitation, largely due to the need to find funds to pay tribute to the Horde. The transition of the southern and western Russian lands under Lithuanian rule also did not contribute to the development of mature forms of feudalism, as the Grand Duchy of Lithuania was an early feudal state (formed in the XIII century). Besides, this state formation "cut off" North-Eastern Russia (which became the core of the Russian centralized state formation) from Central and Western Europe, where XIII-XIV centuries were the time of transition to the dominance of the senorial system, intensive development of trade and cities".

By the end of the XV century, under Ivan III, the North-Eastern and North-Western Russian lands were united into a centralized state with a center in Moscow. Formation of the Russian centralized state chronologically coincides with formation of the centralized monarchies in some countries of the Western Europe. But in social and economic relation Russia was at an earlier stage of development. In the Western Europe of the XIV-XV Eve. - the time of dominance of senorial relations, weakening of personal dependence of peasants, strengthening of cities. In Russia, however, state and feudal forms still prevailed, the relations of personal dependence of peasants on feudal lords were at the stage of formation, cities did not play a significant role. Therefore, there were no sufficient socio-economic prerequisites for the formation of a unified state. In general, the period from the middle of the XIII century to the end of the XVI century. In general, the period from the middle of the XIII century to the end of the XVI century (when the serfdom system was being formed) can be described as an epoch of social shift. There was formed a special type of feudal society, different from the pan-European one, which can be defined as autocratic-state serfdom. In addition to the autocracy and serfdom, its essential feature was the hypertrophied role of the state, and the strict dependence on which were not only the direct producers, but also representatives of the ruling class.

Under the domination of the feudal landownership and the presence of strong serfs, this period took a whole history, an era. Capitalist relations developed very slowly and only in the 19th century developed so much that it led to the fall of serfdom. In comparison with the advanced Western countries feudal Russia remained a backward country. Complicated processes of social and economic development caused further aggravation of class struggle. Mass exodus of peasants from landlords to the south of the country, rapid growth of Cossacks, deep social contradictions in the cities caused numerous antifeudal performances.

Private feudal land ownership in the city ("white slobodas") slowed down the development of planting, because private craftsmen were dangerous competitors to the "black" planting people, driven by the burden of the state and numerous taxes. Property and social stratification took place in the Posad community itself; a group of so-called "big" or "best" people stood out and concentrated in their hands considerable material affinities. In addition, the whole village was against "white slobodas" and heavy feudal oppression. Interests of economic development of the city demanded destruction of constraints and restrictions of crafts and trade activity of planting people. Attracting to its side the top of the merchant and creating a purely feudal privileged corporations of "guests", "living room" and "cloth" hundreds, the government helped bring the top of the merchant with the feudal aristocracy. By attracting merchants and the tops of the peasants to the civil service, the Government distracted them from fishing and trade, which hindered the beginning of the process of so-called initial accumulation.

There is a strengthening of financial oppression due to an increase in direct and indirect taxes. New taxes were introduced - "big yam money", "strelets money" and others. By the mid 17th century, direct taxes from the population had doubled as compared to the 2nd half of the 16th century.

17 в. - It's a time of great popular movements. The uprising led by the Don Cossack Stepan Razin was one of the most significant. The uprising began on the Don, where the peasants - the fugitives from the serfdom - flocked. There were also wealthy, "house" Cossacks on the Don, but the main mass was made up of representatives of the Cossack poor - "Golytuba". Its leader was Stepan Razin. The beginning of the uprising was a voyage along the Volga River in 1667. Differences attacked the royal and merchant caravans, dealt with the royal servants, and workers were taken into their detachments. Caravans of rich Persian vessels were captured in the Caspian Sea, which raised the prestige of Razin. In May 1670 Razin units took Tsaritsyn, Astrakhan, Saratov and Samara. Tsarist voivodeships were killed or expelled from these cities. In detachments to Razin not only Russian serfs, but also peoples of the Volga region - Mordva, Chuvashes, Mari, which were strongly oppressed by imperial authorities flocked. It seemed to the rebellious peasants that their main goal was to destroy their local boyar and landowner, but the main enemy of the peasants was the whole serfdom with the main landowner - the Tsar - at the head. But the peasants thought that instead of a landowner hostile to them, it was possible to plant a "good" for the peasantry, a good king. Brightly flashed in one place, the peasant uprising immediately extinguished. The rebels did not have a single plan of action, they were poorly trained in military affairs, poorly armed. The Tsarist government moved huge military forces and the most experienced voivodeship to Razin. The rebels resisted heroically, but the uprising was crushed. Rich Cossacks gave Razin to the authorities, and in 1671 he was executed.

In the 17th century the process of initial capital accumulation took place in Russia at the initial stage. The peculiarity of this process was that it took place in the atmosphere of domination of feudal serfdom relations, which determined its duration and slowness. There was no such wide expropriation of peasantry in

Russia as in England. "Nevertheless, the growth of commodity-money relations, the formation of the all-Russian market, the increased tax burden ruined the peasantry, pulled it off the ground. A considerable number of craftsmen were also ruined. Some of the fleeing and ruined peasants and artisans - the people of Posad - were already employed.

At the same time, some merchants and wealthy peasants and artisans accumulated quite large amounts of money in their hands. The main source of this wealth was trade, primarily the non-equivalent exchange with the peoples of Siberia, which was clearly colonial in nature. Contracts and repayments, which the city top received from the state, were also of some importance for the initial accumulation. The nascent initial accumulation of capital was the basis for the emergence in Russia of elements of capitalist production relations.

In the 17 c. regional bread markets were formed (in Vyatka land, Velikiy Ustyug etc.). In cities the process of transformation of craftsmen into small commodity producers increased. In the 17 c. there was also enlargement of small manufacture accompanied by application of hired labour. Important phenomenon of economical development of Russia in the 17 c. was appearance of manufactory production (iron-making plants in the area of Tula and Kashira, later Olonetsk plants, glassworks near Moscow etc., and also Cannon Yard founded in the end of the 15 c., Money yard, Khamovny yard) with use of free-lance and serf labour. Hired labour was also used in salt industry, river transport. Trade with the countries of the West and the East (export of raw materials and handicrafts, import of manufactured goods and metals) increased significantly. Domestic trade was also growing. Moscow became the center of all-Russian market relations. In the 17 c. the growth of merchandise-money relations also affected the development of agriculture. Peasant farms became more connected with the market which contributed to differentiation of peasants. Some large feudal farms (e.g. boyar V. I. Morozov, etc.) also developed industrial business (potash production, distillery, etc.).

Russia, like other European countries of the 18th century, embarked on the path of modernization. This process was initiated by the reforms of Peter the Great, which covered many areas of society.

What were the prerequisites for Peter's reforms in politics?

1. Russia was a backward country, which posed a serious threat to the national independence of the Russian people.

2. The industry developed, but its structure was serfdom, and especially in terms of volume and technical equipment, was significantly inferior to that of Western European countries.

3. Farming was characterized by routine farming methods and was based on serfs' forced labour.

4. The Russian army, in large part, consisted of a backward nobility militia and Streltsy, poorly trained and armed.

5. Sophisticated state apparatus.

6. 6. Russia was also lagging behind in the field of spiritual culture.

"Immediately upon his accession to the throne, Peter I began reforms, pursuing a single goal: the creation of a powerful defensible state with high international prestige. The implementation of his idea implied the solution of two main problems, on the one hand - the development of market relations, entrepreneurship, raising the general educational level of people, and on the other - the bet was placed on the state apparatus, which led to the total statehood of society".

However, it would be a significant simplification to present Peter the Great's efforts to reform Russia as a consistent implementation of some pre-conceived plan. Most often they were sporadic in the form of reactions to certain emerging circumstances. The most important and direct incentives for Peter the Great's reform efforts were the need to win the Northern War (1700-1721) and, as a result, the need to create a strong army and navy, an effective system of government, a developed economy, etc. As is known, the North War began unsuccessfully for Russia. In November 1700 the Russian army suffered a major defeat near Narva. From that time on, a stormy activity started to create a new type of army - regular. The army began to be manned by recruitment kits: from a certain number of peasant yards one recruit was taken, who was obliged to serve as an ordinary soldier, while his health allowed. Later the service period was limited to 25 years. Officers were recruited from the nobility. All noblemen were obliged to perform military or civil service. The state took full responsibility for the maintenance of soldiers and officers. Thus the army became professional: military service was now the only occupation for soldiers and officers.

To win the war with Sweden, it was necessary to reform not only the army, but also a huge, clumsy state machine. Peter dreamed of creating a state machine that would work clearly, "regularly" as clockwork. Due to a number of circumstances prevailing in the European countries of mentality, which he met in his two foreign travels and close contact with foreigners Kukueva Sloboda, the authoritarian tradition of power in Russia, as well as the rationalistic warehouse of his mind, Peter I believed in the enormous capabilities of the state apparatus. It seemed to him that he would change in a rational way the activity of the state apparatus, and the life of the whole society would change. Especially in a country where state power suppressed society, and the will of the monarch was the law, it was not difficult to believe in the power of the order. Therefore, Peter I, being a man of strong will, accustomed to universal obedience, believed that only he alone knows what the country needs. The logical consequence of this was the reform of the state apparatus. In 1711, the Senate, the supreme body of state power, was created, which replaced the Boyar Duma. Senators were appointed by the king. At the head of the Senate was a prosecutor general. In 1718-1721 the orders were liquidated, and instead of them the boards were established. The main feature of the system of management through boards was a clear division of functions between them. The work order of the collegiums was determined by special regulations, and the general principles of the central government bodies were set out in the General Regulations.

In1708-1710 a new administrative division was created in Russia. The whole country was divided into eight provinces, headed by governors with full executive and judicial power at the local level.

Maintaining a regular army and a sprawling state apparatus required gigantic resources. One of the ways to get these funds was considered tax reform.

In pre-Peter times, the yard was taxed, equal to the number of tax paid and 10 and 20 inhabitants of the yard. Peter introduced the per capita tax - now the tax was levied on one man (soul). A per capita census was conducted to record the taxpayers, and then its revision. Since then, periodic censuses (audits) have become a norm of Russian life.

Essential to the spiritual life of Russians was the reform of church administration. This reform affected very sensitive aspects of Russian life and was therefore carried out gradually. In 1700 Patriarch Andrian died. Peter I decided to postpone the choice of a new patriarch, and to manage church affairs in accordance with the "Spiritual Regulations" in 1721 was established the state board of the Holy Synod. Thus, the patriarchate was in fact abolished (although no such decision was taken officially). The Synodal period of the Church's activity began, which lasted until August 1917. The Synod was engaged in the property affairs of the church, the appointment of senior officials - diocesan bishops, performed coordination functions in the field of religious and moral education and upbringing.

The establishment of the Holy Synod meant the complete subordination of the spiritual power to the secular, the church became one of the state institutions and had to serve the state interests directly. This had a negative impact on the spiritual life of Russian society. The Orthodox Church was administratively limited and mothballed and humbled its position as a minister to the regime. Unlike in the West, where the Catholic Church played an independent political role, and moreover, dictated its will to political regimes. For example, the Catholic Church had a decisive influence on the formation of political power. For this reason, Russian clergy never acted as spiritual leaders who would lead society forward. On the contrary, the Church actively opposed all innovations.

The creation of new power structures ends with the proclamation of Peter the Great in 1721 as emperor, i.e. head of the secular and spiritual spheres of life. Never before had the head of the Russian state had such full authority. "...his majesty an autocratic monarch, who should not give anybody in the world an answer about his affairs". It should be especially noted that this is a conscious choice of Peter, as he absolutely does not perceive the European social structure, which provided for the autonomy of society from power. The system of power, created by Peter I, is called absolutism.

In fact, since Peter the Great Russia has received a "catching up" economy, when all the power of the state with variable success was directed to "catching up" the stone-west, the latter, understandably, in every way prevented it (who needs a competitor filled with resources!), in this regard we can trace the policy of Catherine II, Alexander II, Witte, Stolypin, the course of "catching up and overtake" the Soviet power. However, Russia's reformatory path was interrupted not only by the braking of the ruling elite and the lack of inner peace, but, most importantly, the peace of the outside. Russia was constantly in a state of "cold" and "hot" war.

The problems of industrialization were set as early as 1925, when the main goals of the Soviet economy were defined:

- elimination   of the technical   and economic backwardness   of the country;

- to achieve economic independence;

- to build a powerful defense industry;

priority development of basic industries (fuel, metallurgical, chemical and machine building).

These tasks were hampered by a lack of material and financial resources, forcing the leadership to move towards an increasingly centralized allocation of resources available in the country. This solution was pushed not only by the experience of civil war, but also by Marxist attitudes to the existence of planned economy under socialism.

The main source of funds allocated for the first five-year period was "internal savings", obtained primarily from the "consumer asceticism" of the population. The country was intensively exporting raw materials, food - bread, butter, sugar, consumption of which by own population was sharply limited. Oil, gold, wood were exported, treasures of Russian museums were sold out.

At the same time, foreign companies provided significant assistance in supplying the latest equipment.

Heavy industry output grew 2.8 times over the five-year period, while machine building output grew 4 times. Dneproges, Magnitogorsk and Kuznetsk metallurgical plants, large coal mines in Donbass and Kuzbass, Stalingrad and Kharkov tractor plants, Moscow and Gorky automobile plants were put into operation, traffic on the Turkestan-Siberian railway opened.

The implementation of grandiose industrialization required a fundamental reorganization of the agricultural sector. In western countries, the agrarian revolution, i.e. the system of improving agricultural production, preceded the industrial revolution, and therefore it was generally easier to supply the urban population with products. In the USSR, both of these processes had to be implemented simultaneously. At the same time, the village was seen not only as a source of food, but also as an important channel for replenishing financial resources for industrialization.

Two interrelated violent processes took place in the village: the establishment of kolkhozes and procrastination. The liquidation of kulak farms was aimed primarily at providing collective farms with material resources.

Collectivization has created the necessary conditions for the implementation of industrialization jump plans. It provided the city with a huge number of workers, while eliminating agrarian overpopulation, allowed, with a significant reduction in the number of employees, to maintain agricultural production at a level that does not allow long-term hunger, provided industry with the necessary raw materials. Collectivization not only created conditions for pumping funds from village to city for the needs of industrialization, but also fulfilled an important political and ideological task, destroying the last islet of market economy - private farming.

The centralization of all internal sources made it possible to achieve unprecedented results in industrial production in an unusually short time. The growth rate of heavy industry was 2-3 times higher than in Russia before the First World War. In terms of absolute volumes of industrial production, the USSR at the end of the 30s ranked second in the world after the USA. Lagging behind the developed capitalist countries in per capita industrial production was reduced. Average annual growth rates of industrial production were the highest in the world, ranging from 10 to 17%.

The qualitative backwardness of the Soviet industry was overcome in a number of areas. The USSR became one of the countries able to produce any kind of industrial products and do without importing essential goods. The economic potential created in the 30s made it possible to deploy a diversified military-industrial complex on the eve of the war and during the war, the production of which exceeded the best world models in many respects.

But the leap in the development of heavy industry was bought at the price of lagging behind other sectors of the economy, first of all light industry and agrarian sector; super-centralization of economic life; limiting the scope of market mechanisms; full subordination of the producer to the state; increasing use of non-economic coercive measures.

During the Great Patriotic War of 1941-45 the Soviet people had to make serious sacrifices in order to defeat the enemy. Only the direct damage caused by fascist armies to the Soviet state and population during the war, on the territory which has undergone occupation, has made (at pre-war state prices) 679 billion rbl.

In difficult wartime conditions, the Communist Party and the Soviet government took great care to meet the household needs of workers and to supply the population with food and industrial goods. Large housing construction was under way in the eastern part of the country. Having defeated the enemy, the Soviet people under the leadership of the Communist Party healed the deep wounds caused by the war in a short period of time, and managed not only to restore the pre-war level of development of the national economy, but also to far surpass it. On this basis, the living standards of workers in the USSR have been significantly improved.

In the post-war years, the material and cultural standard of living of workers has been raised by raising the incomes of workers, employees and peasants, lowering the prices of consumer goods, increasing public spending on social and cultural activities, etc.

At the end of 1947, the Soviet state liquidated the card system introduced during the war and carried out monetary reform. At the same time, high prices in commercial trade were abolished and unified state reduced retail prices for food and industrial goods were introduced. Workers' and employees' wages, as well as peasants' income from public procurement and other labour income for all segments of the population, were not affected by the reform and continued to be paid in new money in the same amounts.

During 8 years (1947-54) the prices for mass consumption goods were reduced 7 times. As a result, in 1954, compared to 1947, prices decreased on average by more than 2.3 times, including 2.6 times for food products and 1.9 times for industrial goods. The amount of goods which in 1947 could be bought for 1,000 rubles was sold for 430 rubles in 1954. In 1954, the prices of some of the most important goods were lower than the pre-war 1940 prices. At the same time, it should be taken into account that cash wages of workers and employees in the postwar years more than doubled, which ensured the growth of real wages.

The Decree of the Council of Ministers of the USSR, the CPSU Central Committee and the All-Union Central Council of Trade Unions from January 1, 1957 increased the wages of low-paid workers and employees. Workers and employees working directly at industrial enterprises, construction sites, transport and communications enterprises were paid at least 300-350 rubles per month, while other workers and employees in cities and work settlements - at least 300 rubles, and in rural areas - at least 270 rubles per month. At the same time, it was abolished the collection of income tax and tax from bachelors, single and small family citizens - workers, employees and students, receiving wages or scholarships of up to 370 rubles per month.

As a result of this regulation, the wages of low-paid groups of workers and employees have increased by an average of approximately 33%. In March 1957, taxes on workers and employees receiving wages were reduced to 450 rubles per month.

The party and the government undertook a number of activities in the post-war years to increase the income of collective farmers. In 1953, state procurement prices for livestock products, vegetables and potatoes were raised. The procurement prices for cattle and poultry, which were delivered to the state as obligatory supplies, were increased more than 5.5 times, for milk and butter - 2 times, for potatoes - 2.5 times. At the same time, procurement prices (i.e. prices at which peasants can sell their surplus to the state) have been raised: procurement prices for meat - by 30% on average, for milk - 1.5 times. In August 1953, a new law on agricultural tax was adopted, which reduced the amount of tax in 1953 by 43 per cent, and in 1954 - by 2.5 times compared to 1952. The remaining arrears under the agricultural tax of previous years were completely removed from the personal subsidiary farms of collective farmers, all the arrears of pasta and potatoes were written off. The Decree of the Central Committee of the CPSU and the Council of Ministers of the USSR of July 4, 1957 abolished mandatory supplies: to the state all agricultural products by the farms of collective farmers, members of fishing and fishing artels, members of the artel of cooperation of the disabled, farms of workers and employees working on a permanent basis in state enterprises and institutions, cooperative and public organizations living in rural, urban areas and countryside villages.

In the mid-50s, procurement prices for potatoes and vegetables were raised again. All these measures ensured significant growth of natural and monetary incomes of collective farmers.

# Ivan the Terrible - as an example of a Russian autocrat.

*Ivan the Terrible. Portrait of the 16th century. National Museum in Copenhagen.*

The half-century reign of Ivan the Terrible left a deep and dark trace in the history of Russia. The life of the first bearer of the title of Russian Tsar, full of dramatic events, interested many historians and writers. As a man and as a statesman Ivan the Fourth was a complex and controversial personality. A highly educated patron of book printing and the writer himself, the Tsar,

who did much to strengthen and expand the Russian state, he destroyed with his own hands what he had created, and at the same time cruelly persecuted those who owed the success of domestic politics and foreign policy victories.

There are two periods on the board of Ivan 4:

1. a period of success in foreign policy and legislation (it coincides with the activities of the Favourites);

2. "period of madness" (it begins with the fall of Sylvester and Adashev).

R.Y.Whipper expressed his original thoughts about Grozny in his time: "If Ivan the Terrible had died in 1566 at the time of his greatest success on the western front, his preparation for the final conquest of Livonia, historical memory would have given him the name of a great conqueror, the creator of the world's largest power, like Alexander the Great. The blame for the loss of the Baltic region he conquered would have fallen on his successors at that time: after all, Alexander's premature death was the only thing that saved him from a direct encounter with the collapse of the empire he had created. In case of such an early end, at the 36th year of his life, Ivan the Fourth would have remained in the historical tradition surrounded by the glory of a remarkable reformer, organizer of military service class, founder of the administrative centralization of the Moscow power. His vices, his executions would have been forgiven him just as his offspring forgave Alexander the Great his depravity and atrocities".

The personality of Tsar Ivan IV (the Terrible) has always attracted to himself, which is called negative charm. It was a bright personality, individuality, not mediocrity. Ivan the Terrible has remained in history the embodiment of despotism and tyranny of the Russian autocracy. Raised in the years of boyar rule, from the age of 8, deprived of his mother, he experienced the horrors of boyar quarrels and boyar rampage. It saw blood and flattery, very early began to think about authority, that it sovereign of Moscow and All Russia.

Ivan was born on August 25, 1530 in the family of Grand Duke Vasily III. Being three years old, he lost his father, and at the age of less than eight he lost his mother Elena Glinskaya. His four-year-old brother Yuri could not share children's amusement with him. The child was deaf and mute from birth. According to his father's will, the administration of the state passed into the hands of the boyars, who were to transfer power to the prince when he came of age.

After the death of Grand Duchess Elena Glinskaya, power passed into the hands of members of the Semboyarsk region, who hurriedly dealt with Prince Ovchina. The guardians were unanimous in their hatred of the temporary worker, but their agreement soon came to an end.

With the death of Andrei Staritsky, Prince Vasily Vasilyevich Shuisky became the oldest among the guardians. This boyar, who was more than 50 years old, married Princess Anastasia, cousin of the young Grand Duke Ivan. Becoming a member of the Grand-Ducal family, Prince Vasily wanted to arrange a life decent to his new position, from the old courtyard he moved to live in the courtyard of Staritsky.

While there was a struggle for power between the feudals, Ivan, in his own words, grew into "negligence". Boyars took little care of the teenager. And he and his younger brother Yuri endured the need even in dress and food. All this hardened and outraged the teenager, already aware of what is happening. Therefore, Ivan for life has maintained a bad attitude towards guardians. In his letters, he did not hide his irritation against them. Boyars did not devote Ivan in their affairs, but watched his affections and hurried to remove from the palace of possible favorites.

When Ivan reached adulthood, he remembered his orphanhood more than once. His ink was turned into bile when he described the resentment caused to him - an abandoned orphan - by the boyars. A feeling of abandonment and loneliness hit the orphan's soul early and deeply. Ugly scenes of boyar willfulness and violence, among which Ivan grew up, turned his timidity into nervous timidity. The child experienced a terrible nervous shock when the boyars of Shuisky once at dawn broke into his bedroom, woke him up and frightened him. Over the years, in Ivan developed suspicion and deep distrust of people.

Ivan was rapidly developing physically and at the age of 13 he looked like a real mayor. An ambassadorial order officially announced abroad that the great sovereign "in the age of man enters, and the growth of a perfect man is, and with God's will is already thinking of the marriage season accepted. The clerks described the external signs of a grown up young man quite accurately, but they vainly attributed to him the degree of thought of marriage. The teenager is very little reminiscent of the old boy, who grew up in "captivity" and strictness, freed from the care and authority of the oldest boyars, the Grand Duke indulged in wild amusement and games, which deprived him of childhood.

The surrounding people were amazed by Ivan's rampage and furious temper. At the age of 12, he climbed into the island terems and shove cats and dogs from there "creature of the dumb". At the age of 14, he started "dropping men". Bloody amusement was the "great sovereign"'s pleasure. The boy was desperately disfigured. With the vataga of his peers, children of the most noble boyars, he traveled through the streets and squares of the city, trampled the people on horses, beat and robbed the common people "jumping and running everywhere ungratefully.

As the Grand Duke grew up, intrigues intensified, the boyars more and more involved in their strife. Vorontsov's attempt to gain confidence in Ivan ended sadly for him. Ivan well remembered how in his presence there was a scuffle in the Duma, when Andrei Shuisky and his supporters rushed with their fists on the boyar Vorontsov, began to beat him, cut off his dress, "to take out of the hut would want to kill. After that he was exiled to Kostroma, despite Ivan's intercession.

The 13-year-old "autocrat" hasn't forgiven his resentment, though. Not 3 months after the incident in the Duma one of the "caressers" taught the Grand Duke to execute Andrei Shuisky. Prince Shuisky, who stood at that time in the head of the department, was on his orders captured by the Grand Ducal dogs and killed, and his advisers were sent into exile in the cities. Psari attacked the boyar near the palace at the Kuryatny gate, the killed lay for 2 hours "From those places - recorded by the chronicler - became the boyars of the sovereign fear of having and obedience.

The fall of Shuisky, eventually used the uncle of the Grand Duke - Princes Glinsky. In essence, the reign of Glinskys differed little from that of Shuisky; their people robbed the population lawlessly. Boyars disposed of state land fund in their favour, state treasury was plundered.

It took long and long years before Ivan IV achieved obedience from the boyars, while he himself became an instrument in the hands of the courtiers.

The situation created by the boyars as a result of their "outrage and complacency" posed a serious threat to the integrity of the state and should have prompted attempts to consolidate power by those groups of the state classes who feared the collapse of the state unity. The first such attempt was made by Metropolitan Macarius. He was believed to be an ardent supporter of strong autocratic power. Under the undoubted influence of Makariy was the political ideology of Ivan the Terrible. Macarius probably belonged to the idea of marriage to the kingdom of young Ivan. This act was to not only increase the international importance of the Russian state, but also strengthen the shattered central power.

When Ivan turned 16, the Boyar Duma and the Metropolitan crowned him to the kingdom. The assumption of the royal title marked the beginning of his independent rule.

The wedding of the kingdom took place on January 16, 1547. Everything was done to give it as much brilliance and solemnity as possible.

There was a bell ringing above Moscow. It rang in all the Kremlin cathedrals, secondary to them were peripheral churches and monasteries. They announced to Moscow inhabitants about solemn event - wedding of young sovereign Grand Duke of All Russia Ivan Vasilyevich on kingdom.

In the Kremlin, the procession was moving slowly and smoothly. From the Grand Ducal Palace it was headed for the main Moscow Cathedral of the Assumption of the Virgin Mary, rebuilt under Ivan III, the grandfather of the present Grand Duke. In heavy fur coats, sable, ermine, squirrel, covered with oriental silks with bright divorces, Italian velvet, or Flemish cloth, the boyars were moving smoothly. Mesmerized by the splendor of the procession and the seriousness of what was happening, the crowd froze. Is it a joke, a wedding to the kingdom. Moscow has never seen such a thing.

During the long, according to the custom of the Orthodox Church, the Metropolitan laid a cross, a crown and bars on Ivan. By the mouths of the metropolitan, the program of the Tsar's activities was outlined: in union with the Church, which was now declared the "mother" of the Tsar's power, the Tsar had to strengthen the "court and truth" within the country, to fight for the expansion of the state.

At the end of the wedding ceremony the Grand Duke became "the God's King". On a scarlet velvet flowing like a stream of blood, on a dazzling white snow, went to his choirs the first Russian tsar, who carried this title on legitimate, from the point of view of that world foundations.

The capital of the state, Moscow, has now been decorated with a new title - it became a "reigning city", and the Russian land - the Russian kingdom. But for the peoples of Russia, one of the most tragic periods in its history began. It was the "time of Ivan the Terrible".

At the time of reforms, Ivan's personal influence was moderated by the authority of his advisers. In his young years, the Tsar, together with his elected advisors, led a bold foreign and domestic policy, the aim of which was, on the one hand, to put in order the legislation, arrange regional administration and attract elected people from different estates to it, on the other hand, to expand the borders of the state in the East and West, to achieve the Baltic Sea coast and strengthen ties with Western Europe.

These complex tasks required a long and painstaking work, which did not suit Tsar Ivan. By introducing oprichnina he sought to solve the problems of completing the centralization of the state, overcome the resistance of the boyar opposition, to achieve the strengthening of personal power and to separate the enemies. And if Ivan IV's father and grandfather skillfully attracted to their side the former independent princes, giving them generous promises and real privileges, the Terrible brought unpredictable cruelty and despotism into this process.

He finally got rid of the old advisers and the boyar care. It would seem that the king has finally reached an unlimited power, which he was harassing. But this impression seems to be exaggerated. Oprichnina was Grozny's favourite child, but she was not the fruit of his mind and energy alone. In the most important periods of oprichnina next to Tsar Ivan invariably stands a whole plethora of figures of the practical warehouse with the domination of terrifying people. "On the contrary, it is the domination of people who themselves are frightened. Terror is, for the most part, a useless cruelty, committed for their own comfort by people who are themselves afraid.

Bloody terror has put a deep stamp on all aspects of political life. Low worship and glorification have never blossomed so lavishly. Trick-or-treaters and co-workers praised the wisdom and infallibility of the ruler without any measure.

Under the influence of fear and inordinate praise Grozny, despite all his natural intelligence, increasingly lost perspective, became intolerant of any contradiction and stubbornly made a mistake for a mistake. In the end, he surrounded himself with dubious, unscrupulous careerists and executioners.

Oprichnina created the appearance of the omnipotence of the Moscow autocrat. But in the realm of oprichnyi terror ruler himself became a toy in the hands of adventurers like Malyuta Skuratov.

In his youth Ivan was fond of religion, in his mature years he became a complete fanatic. Many of his cruel and incomprehensible actions had religious fanaticism as an incentive.

# Brief Chronicle

859 Northern Slavic tribes which paid then a tribute to Vikings, or Normans (in opinion of the majority of historians, to descendants from Scandinavia), drove them out of the sea. However soon after these events in Novgorod internecine struggle began. To stop the clashes, the Novgorodians decided to invite Viking princes as a force standing over the opposing groups.

862 Prince Rurik and his two brothers were called to Russia by Novgorodians, having put the beginning of Russian princely dynasty.

863 The uprising against the Vikings in Novgorod was led by Vadim the Brave, who after defeating the rebels was killed.

864 Rurik Askold and Dir take over Kiev.

863 Askold is on a military expedition to the Half Men.

866 Askold and Dir's campaign to Tsargrad.

879 Death in Novgorod Rurik. The power has been transferred to a relative or voivode Oleg.

882 Date of formation of the Old Russian state when prince Oleg who has grasped after Rurik's death authority in Novgorod (some chroniclers name it voivode Rurik), has undertaken a campaign to Kiev. Having killed Askold and Dir, who reigned there, he united the northern and southern lands into a single state for the first time. Since the capital was moved from Novgorod to Kiev, this state is often called Kievan Rus. Oleg's campaign to Byzantium.

883 Tributed to the Drevlyans.

884 The Conquest of Oleg the North.

885 The conquest of the Tiberias, the streets and the Radomites. Conflict with the Khazar Kaganate.

889 Badjanak invasion in the south.

898 Kiev has paid off from Ugric tribes which have left on the West.

907, 911, 944 - the first treaties of Russia with Byzantium

912-945 - board of prince Igor

957 - Princess Olga's embassy in Constantinople

962-972 - board of prince Svyatoslav

967-971 - Svyatoslav's campaigns on the Danube.

980-1015 - board of prince Vladimir the Sacred

988 - introduction of Christianity in Russia

1019-1054 - Board of Prince Yaroslav the Wise

1051 - election of Hilarion as metropolitan of All Russia.

Mid-11th century - foundation of Kievo-Pecherskiy monastery.

1054-1073, 1076-1078 - board of prince Izyaslav I.

1068, 1113 - uprisings in Kiev

1072 - compilation of Yaroslavich's "Russian Truth".

1073-1076 - board of prince Svyatoslav

1078-1093 - board of prince Vsevolod.

1097 - Congress of Princes in Lyubich

1111 - a crusade of princes led by Vladimir Monomakh.
antipolovtsev

1113-1125 - Board of Prince Vladimir Monomakh in Kiev

Beginning of the 12th century - "The Tale of Bygone Years."

1125-1132 - Board of Prince Mstislav the Great in Kiev

1125-1157 - Board of Prince Yuri Dolgoruky in Suzdal

1136 - The expulsion of Prince Vsevolod from Novgorod.

30th XII century - beginning of political fragmentation of Russia

1153-1187 - Board of Prince Yaroslav Ostromir in Galicia.

1157-1174 - board of prince Vladimir Bogolyubsky in Vladimir

1176-1212 Reigning of Vsevolod Yurievich the Big Nest in the Vladimir-Suzdal land

1199-1205 Roman Mstislavich's reign in the Principality of Galicia-Volhynia

1206 Proclamation of Temuchin to the Head of the Mongolian Power and acceptance of the name of Genghis Khan by him

1216-1218 Reigning Constantine Vsevolodovich in the Vladimir-Suzdal land

1216 Thc Battle of Lipetsk

1218-1228 Reigning of Yury Vsevolodovich in the Vladimir-Suzdal land

1219-1221 Mongols conquest of Central Asia

1223 The Battle of Kalka River

1227 Death of Genghis Khan

1237-1238 Batyi invasion of North-Eastern Russia

March 4, 1238 Battle of the City River

1238-1246 Grand Duchy of Yaroslav Vsevolodovich

1239-1264 Daniel Romanovich's reign on the Galician land

July 15, 1240 Victory of Novgorod Prince Alexander Yaroslavich over Swedes on the Neva River

1240-1242 Batu Khan's Campaign to Southern Russia, Poland, Hungary and Moravia

December 6, 1240 The capture of Kiev by the Tatars

April 5, 1242 Ice Battle

Around 1243 Golden Horde formation.

1249-1252 Andrei Yaroslavich's Grand Duchy

1257-1258 Horde census of Russian land

1259-1263 The Grand Duchy of Alexander Nevsky

1265 (?) -1300 The existence of the Black Sea ulus Nogai.

1276-1303 Daniel Alexandrovich reigns in Moscow

1300 - Transfer of Metropolitan Maxim from Kiev to Vladimir

1301 Joining Kolomna to Moscow

1302 The annexation of the Principality of Pereyaslavl to Moscow

1303-1325 Yuri Danilovich's Reigning in Moscow

1305 - Creation of the all-Russian annalistic vault in Tver

1309 Transfer of Metropolitan Peter from Kiev to Vladimir-on-Klyazma

1316-1341 The reign of Gedimin in Lithuania

1318-1322 Grand Duchy of Yuri Danilovich (Moscow)

1326 Transfer of the metropolis from Vladimir to Moscow

1327 Uprising against the Nutcracker in Tver

1328-1341 Grand Duchy of Ivan Kalita in Moscow

1341-1353 The Grand Duchy of Simeon the Proud

1345-1377 Olgerd's reign in the Grand Duchy of Lithuania and Russia

1349 The seizure of Galicia by the Polish King Casimir

1353-1359 The Grand Duchy of Ivan Ivanovich the Gracious

1359-1389 The Grand Duchy of Dmitry Donskoy in Moscow. The label for the Grand Duchy was issued by the Horde in 1362.

1367-1368 Construction of the stone Kremlin in Moscow

1377 Beginning of Jagiel's reign in the Grand Duchy of Lithuania and Russia (king of Poland from 1386)

August 11, 1378 Battle of Voga

September 8, 1380 Kulikovskaya Battle

1382 The burning of Moscow by Tokhtamysh

1385 Union of the Grand Duchy of Lithuania and Russia with Poland

1389-1425 The Grand Duchy of Vasily I Dmitrievich

1392-1430 The Duchy of Vitovt in the Grand Duchy of Lithuania and Russia

1399 Battle of Vorskla

1408 The Occasion of Yedigey

July 15, 1410 The Battle of Grunwald

1413 The urban union of Poland and the Grand Duchy of Lithuania and Russia

1425-1462 Grand Duchy of Basil II Vasilyevich the Dark

1439 The Florentine Union

1440-1492 Duchy of Kazimir Yagailovich in the Grand Duchy of Lithuania and Russia (king of Poland from 1447).

1462-1505 Grand Duchy of Ivan III Vasilyevich

1472 Marriage of Ivan III Vasilyevich with Greek Tsarevna Sophia Paleologica

1478 Accession of Novgorod to the Moscow State

1480 "Standing" on the Ugra River. The death of khan Ahmat

1485 Accession of the Principality of Tver to the Moscow State

1485-1516 Construction of new Kremlin walls in Moscow

1497 Trial judge Ivan III

1500-1503, 1507-1508, 1512-1522, 1534-1537 - Russian-Lithuanian wars

1500 - The Battle of Buckets

1505-1533 - board of Vasily III

1533-1584 - reign of Ivan IV the Terrible

1547 - wedding of Ivan the Terrible to his reign

1549 - the first Zemsky Cathedral

50th XVI century - reforms of the Favorite Rada

1550 - court officer Ivan the Terrible

1551 - One hundred heads cathedral

1552 - accession to Kazan

1556 - accession of Astrakhan

1558-1583 - Livonian War

1564 - Ivan Fyodorov published the first printed book in Russia

1565-1572 - oprichnina

1572 - The Battle of Moldova

1581-1585 - Ermak's campaign to Siberia

1584-1598 - the board of Fedor

80-90s of the XVI century - decrees on consolidation of peasants.

1589 - election of Job as the first patriarch of Russia

1598-1605 - Board of Boris Godunov

1605-1606 - Board of Falsdmitry I

1606-1610 - Board of Vasily Shuisky

1609-1611 - defense of Smolensk

1611 - formation of the First militia

1612 - establishment of the Second militia, liberation of Moscow

1613 - election of Mikhail Romanov as king at the Zemsky Cathedral.

1613-1645 - board of Mikhail

1632-1634 - The Smolensk War

1645-1676 - board of Alexey

1648, 1650, 1662 - urban uprisings

1649 - Cathedral Layout

1653 - the beginning of the church reform of Patriarch Nikon.

1654-1667 - Russian-Polish War

1666-1667 - church cathedral

1667-1671 - Uprising led by Stepan Razin

1676-1681 - Russian-Turkish war (Chigirin campaigns).

1676-1682 - Fedor's board of directors

1682 - Streltsy Uprising

1682-1689 - board of Sophia

1687, 1689 - Crimean campaigns by V. Golitsyn.

1687 - Opening of the Slavic-Greco-Latin Academy

1682-1725 - reign of Peter 1 the Great

1695, 1696 - Azov campaigns

1696 - decree on the establishment of a fleet in Russia

1696-1698 - Great Embassy to Western Europe

1699 - establishment of the first Russian Order of St. Andrew the First Called

1700-1721 - Northern War

1700 - dissolution of the patriarchate

1703 - foundation of St. Petersburg

1707-1708 - rebellion led by K.A. Bulavin

June 27, 1709 - The Battle of Poltava

1711 - establishment of the Senate; Prut campaign

1714 - The Battle of Gangut

1721 - proclamation of Russia as an empire

1722 - publication of "Table of Ranks".

1725-1727 - board of Catherine I.

1725 - establishment of the Academy of Sciences

1727-1730 - board of Peter II

1730-1740 - board of Anna

1735-1739 - Russian-Turkish war

1740-1741 - Board of Ivan VI

1741-1761 - Elizabeth's board of directors

1741-1743 - Russian-Swedish war

17 54 - Cancellation of domestic customs and duties

1755 - establishment of Moscow University

1757 - establishment of the Academy of Arts

1757-1762 - Russia's participation in the Seven Years' War

1759 - Battle of Kunersdorf

1760 - capture by Russian troops of Berlin

1761-1762 - board of Peter III

1762 - Manifesto on the liberty of the nobility

1762-1796 - board of Catherine II

1767 - convening of the commission to draw up a new constitution

1768-1774 - Russian-Turkish war

1770 - the Battles of Riaba Mogila, Larga, Cahul.

1770 - The Battle of Chesmen

1772, 1793, 1795 - sections of the Rzeczpospolita.

1773-1775 - Uprising led by E. V. Lenin. I. Pugachev

1783 - opening of the Russian Academy

1783 - accession of the Crimea (Taurida)

1785 - publication of letters of commendation to the nobility and cities

1787-1791 - Russian-Turkish war

1787-1790 - Russian-Swedish war

1790 - capture of Ishmael

1791 - Battle at Cape Kaliakria

1796-1801 - board of Paul I

1799 - taking the fortress by Korf F. Ushakov

1799 - Italian and Swiss campaigns by A. V. Suvorov.

1801-1825 - board of Alexander I

1803 - decree on free bakers

1804 - opening of Kazan University

1804-1813, 1826-1828 - Russian-Iranian wars.

1805, 1806-1807 - Russia's participation in the wars with Napoleon.

1806-1812 - Russian-Turkish war

1807 - Tilsit World

1808-1809 - Russian-Swedish war, accession of Finland

1812 - Patriotic War

August 26, 1812 - Battle of Borodino

1813-1814 - foreign campaign of the Russian army

1813 - Battle of Leipzig

1814-1815 - Vienna Congress

1817-1864 - Caucasian War

1825 - Decembrist Uprising

1825-1855 - board of Nikolai I

1828-1829 - Russian-Turkish war

1830-1831 - Uprising in Poland, Russian-Polish War

1833 - approval of the Code of Laws of the Russian Empire

1837-1841 - state peasant management reform

П. D. Kiseleva

1839-1843 - financial reform E. F. Kankrin

40-50th of XIX century - disputes between Westerners and Slavophiles.

1851 - opening of railway traffic from Moscow to St. Petersburg.

1853-1856 - Crimean War

September 1854 - August 1855 - defense of Sevastopol.

1855-1881 - rule of Alexander II

1857 - rescript to V. I. Nazimov, beginning of creation of provincial noble committees for development of peasant reform

1858 - establishment of editorial boards

February 19, 1861 - abolition of serfdom.

1864 - land and judicial reforms

60-70s of the XIX century - accession of Central Asia

1870 - urban governance reform

1874 - military reform

1877-1878 - Russian-Turkish war

1878 - Berlin Congress

1881-1894 - board of Alexander III

1885 - Morozovskaya strike

1891 - beginning of Trans-Siberian railway construction.

1891-1893 - registration of the Russian-French Union

1893 - start of industrial lifting

1894-1917 - board of Nicholas II

1897 - monetary reform S.J. Witte

1898 March 1-2 - I Congress of RSDLP in Minsk

1898 - conclusion of the Russian-Chinese convention on the lease of the Liaodong Peninsula with Port Arthur

1900-1903 - economic crisis

1900 - emergence of the monarchist organization "Russian Assembly" in St. Petersburg.

1902 - foundation of the Party of Socialist Revolutionaries (SSR).

1902 - foundation of Liberation magazine in Stuttgart.

1903 July - general strike in the south of Russia

1903 July 17 - August 10 - II Congress of the RSDLP in Brussels and London. The birth of Bolshevism

1903 November 8 - I Congress of "Zemtsev-Constitutionalists" in Moscow.

1904-1905 - Russian-Japanese War

1904 January 3-5 - constituent congress of the "Liberation Union" in St. Petersburg.

1904 July 17 - December 20 - Defence of Port Arthur

1904 November 6-9 - "Private meeting" of Zemstvo officials (First Zemstvo Congress) in St. Petersburg

1904 November - December - "Banquet Campaign"

1904 December 13-31 - general strike of oil workers in Baku

1904-1907 - registration of the "Triple Consent" (Entente) - military and political union of Great Britain, France and Russia

1905 January 9th - "Bloody Sunday." Beginning of the first Russian revolution

1905 April - establishment of the Russian Monarchist Party and monarchist organization "Union of Russian people".

1905 May 12 - June 1 - general strike in Ivanovo-Voznesensk. Formation of the first Council of Working Deputies

1905 May 14-15 - Tsushima Battle

1905 June 14-24 - rebellion on the battleship Potemkin.

1905 July 31 - August 1 - founding congress of the All-Russian Peasant Union in Moscow

1905 August 6 - publication of Manifesto on convocation of representative body - State ("Bulygin") Duma

1905 August 23 (September 5) - Portsmouth Peace Treaty between Russia and Japan

1905 October 7 - the beginning of the All-Russian political strife

1905 October 12-18 - founding congress of the Constitutional Democratic Party (cadets)

1905 October 13 - establishment of the St. Petersburg Council of Working Deputies

1905 October 17 - manifesto of Nicholas II on civil liberties and on granting legislative and supervisory powers to the State Duma

1905 October 19 - reorganization of the Council of Ministers. Transformation of the Council of Ministers into a permanent body - the Government of the Russian Empire

1905 November - creation of monarchic party "Union of Russian people".

1905 November - establishment of the "Union of October 17" (Octoberist party).

1905 November - publication of Manifesto on reduction of redemption payments by half from January 1, 1906 and their termination from January 1, 1907

1905 December 9-19 - Moscow armed uprising

1905 11 December - electoral law on elections to the State Duma

1906 February 20 - "Provisions on the State Duma and the State Council".

1906 April 23 - publication of "Fundamental Laws" of the Russian Empire

1906 April 27 - July 8 - I State Duma

1906 November 9 - Beginning of agrarian reform by P. A. Stolypin

1906 November 9 - issue of a special act allowing the government to take legislative measures in between Duma sessions.

1906 August 19 - Nicholas II approved the law on military field ships.

1907 February 20 - June 2 - II State Duma

1907 June 3 - dissolution of the II State Duma. Adoption of the new electoral law

1907 18 (31) August - Russian-English agreement on the division of spheres of influence in the Middle East

1907 November 1 - 1912 June 9 - III State Duma

1907-1914 - "Russian Seasons" in Paris and London.

1908 - establishment of the Black Hundred Organization "Mikhail Archangel's Union".

1912 July 8 - conclusion of the secret Russian-Japanese convention

1912 15-16 August - conclusion of the Russian-French naval convention

1912 November 15 - 1917 February 25 - IV State Duma

1913 - approval of the "Great Program to Reinforce the Army."

1914 May - August - general strike of workers in St. Petersburg

1914 July 19 (August 1) - Germany declared war on Russia. The beginning of the First World War

1914 July 24 (August 6) - Austria-Hungary declaration of war on Russia

1915 March - April - conclusion of the Russian-English-French agreement on the Black Sea straits

1915 - establishment of military industrial committees and All-Russian zemstvo and city unions

1915 17 August - establishment of "Special Meetings" on defence, food, fuel and transport

August 1915 - formation of the "Progressive Block".

1916 May 22 - July 31 - Brusilovsky breakthrough

1916 December 17 - murder of Grigory Rasputin

1917 26 February - Beginning of the transition of troops to the Revolution

1917 February 27 - the start of activities of the Petrograd Soviet of Workers' and Soldiers' Deputies. Formation of the State Duma Provisional Committee headed by M. Rodzyanko

1917 March 2 - formation of the Provisional Government headed by E. Lvov. Renunciation of Nicholas II from the throne

1917 March 3 - abdication of Grand Duke Mikhail Alexandrovich.

1917 6 May - formation of the 2nd (first coalition) Interim Government

June 1917 - I All-Russian Congress of Soviets of Workers' and Soldiers' Deputies

1917 3-5 July - July events

1917 July 24th - formation of the 3rd Provisional Government

1917 25-28 August - Kornilov's "case"

1917 August 30 - September 24 - Directory government

1917 25 September - formation of the 4th Provisional Government

1917 October 24-25 - October Revolution. Overthrow of the Provisional Government

1917 October 25-26 - II Congress of Soviets. Decrees on peace, on land, creation of the Council of People's Commissars

1917 November 2 - Declaration of the Rights of the Peoples of Russia

1917 12 November - Constituent Assembly elections

1917 December 7 - formation of the Cheka

1918 January 5-6 - convening and dispersal of the Constituent Assembly

1918 March 3 - Russia's Brest World with the Countries of the Fourth Alliance

1918 March 6-8 - VII Congress of the Party. Renaming of RSDLP(b) to RCP(b)

1918 May 25 - beginning of uprising of Czechoslovak Corps

1918 July 5-6 - Left Socialist Uprising in Moscow

1918 July 10 - adoption of the Constitution of the RSFSR

1918 November 11 - Germany's surrender. End of the First World War

1919 March 2-6 - I Congress of the Communist International in Moscow

1920 - Soviet-Polish War

1921 February 28 - March 18 - Uprising in Kronstadt

1921 March 8-16 - X Congress of the RCP(b). Beginning of the transition to napu

1922 April - Stalin's election as General Secretary of the Central Committee of the Russian Communist Party (b)

1922 April-May - Genoa Conference. Normalization of Soviet-German relations

1922 June-August - right-wing Socialist process in Moscow

1922 August - deportation of about 200 prominent figures of Russian intelligentsia abroad

1922 December 30 - I Congress of Soviets of the USSR. Formation of the USSR

1924 January 21 - V.I. Lenin's death

1924 January 31 - approval of the USSR Constitution

1925 December - XIV Congress of the Party. Renaming of RCP(b) to VKP(b). Speech by the "new opposition", headed by L. B. Kamenev and E. E. Vasilyev. Zinoviev .

1928 June - the so-called "Shakhtinskoye Deal".

1928 October - 1932 December - first five-year period

January 1930 - the beginning of a continuous collectivization.

1933-1937 - second five-year plan

1934 December 1 - The murder of S. M. Kirov.

1936 December 5 - adoption of the USSR Constitution

1938 November - removal of NI Ezhov and appointment of LP Beria as head of the NKVD.

1939 July - August - conflict on Khalkhin-Gol r.

August 1939 - negotiations of military delegations of the USSR, England, France

1939 August 23 - Soviet-German non-aggression pact

1939 September 1 - Germany's attack on Poland. The outbreak of World War II

1939 September 28 - Treaty of friendship and border between Germany and the USSR

1939 November - 1940 March - Soviet-Finnish War

1941 June 22 - the beginning of the Great Patriotic War

1941 October - 1942 April - The Battle of Moscow

1942 November 19 - the beginning of the offensive at Stalingrad

1942 November - 1943 November - a fundamental turning point during the war

1942. January - creation of anti-Hitler coalition.

1943 November 28 - December 1 - Tehran Conference of Leaders of USSR, USA and England

January 1944 - lifting the blockade of Leningrad

1944 February - Yalta Conference of Heads of USA, USSR and England

1945 April - May - Battle of Berlin

1945 May 8 - Germany's surrender

1945 July 17 - August 2 - Potsdam Conference of Heads of Government of USSR, USA, England

1945 August 9 - the outbreak of war between the USSR and Japan.

September 2, 1945 - Japan's surrender. End of World War II

1946 March - renaming of the Council of People's Commissars to the Council of Ministers of the USSR

1946 - Failure in Paris of a peace conference on the German question.

1947 - famine after drought 1946

December 1947 - confiscation monetary reform. Cancellation of the card distribution system for food and industrial goods

1947 - formation of the Academy of Arts of the USSR

1948 - formation of communist, pro-Soviet regimes in several countries of Eastern and South-Eastern Europe.

1948 - campaign "against cosmopolitanism".

1948-1951 - implementation of the "Marshall Plan".

1949 - establishment of the Council for Economic Mutual Assistance (CEM).

1949 - formation of the North Atlantic Bloc (NATO).

1949 - severance of diplomatic and economic relations with Yugoslavia.

1949 - Communist victory in China, formation of the People's Republic of China.

1949 - formation of two German states, GDR and FRG.

1949 - Soviet atomic bomb test

1949-1950 - "Leningrad Business"

1947-1951 - administrative dictate in science

1950-1953 - the Korean War

1952 October - XIX Congress of the All-Union Communist Party of Bolsheviks (b), renaming the party into the CPSU

1953 - "The Doctors' Case"

1953 March 5 - death of I. V. Stalin

1953 July - removal from power and arrest of L. P. Beria.

1953 September - election of Khrushchev First Secretary of the CPSU Central Committee. Adoption of the programme for the raising of agriculture

1953 - Soviet hydrogen bomb test

1954 - beginning of development of virgin and fallow lands.

1954 - launch of the first nuclear power plant in the USSR.

1955 May - Establishment of the Warsaw Treaty Organization (IAB)

1955 - normalization of relations with Yugoslavia, establishment of diplomatic relations with Germany

1955 July - adoption of the program of scientific and technical modernization of industry

1953-1955 - commencement of rehabilitation of victims of repressions

1956 February - XX Congress of the CPSU. Report by Khrushchev "On the personality cult and its consequences".

1956 - the abolition of tuition fees for high school, general education, specialized secondary and higher education institutions

1956 June 30 - Resolution of the CPSU Central Committee "On overcoming the cult of personality and its consequences".

1956 - establishment of state old-age pensions for workers and employees

1956 - Antisocialist uprising in Hungary

1957 - commencement of administrative and management reform, establishment of sovnarhosts.

1957 June - attempt to displace Khrushchev. End of the political career of Molotov, Malenkov, Kaganovich.

1957 October - launch of the world's first artificial Earth satellite, dismissal of K. Zhukov from the post of Minister of Defense

1957 July - VI World Festival of Youth and Students in Moscow

1957 - Launch of the world's first nuclear icebreaker "Lenin".

1958 - liquidation of MTS, sale of equipment to collective farms

1959 - January 2 - Launching a space rocket towards the Moon.

January XXI Congress of the CPSU, setting the task of direct construction of communism, the adoption of a seven-year plan for the development of the USSR national economy in 1959-1965.

January 27 - February 5 - Extraordinary XXI Congress of the CPSU, the adoption of the resolution "On control figures of the development of the national economy of the USSR in 1959-1965".

September 12 - Implementation of the second successful Soviet space rocket launch to the Moon. The first atomic icebreaker "Lenin" entered the Neva and went on its first flight.

October 4 - Implementation of the third launch of the Soviet space rocket, which photographed the back side of the Moon.

May 1960 - spy flight of G. Powers, the beginning of a new round of the Cold War.

The first All-Union meeting of the foremost competition for the title of brigades and strikers of communist labor.

August 19 - A Soviet spacecraft raids the Earth and returns it to the specified area of the USSR.

November 15 - Decree of the Council of Ministers of the USSR "On the new golden content of the ruble and the ruble appreciation against foreign currencies.

# Sociocultural characteristics of Russian society

On the Russian character of N. Losky, a famous Russian philosopher, wrote that he is a remarkable combination of masculine nature and feminine softness. "Who lived in the village and came into contact with the peasants, the one who probably has the living memories of this beautiful combination of courage and softness in his mind" (Lossky I.O. Conditions of absolute good. M., 1991. e. 289).

Rough history has brought up in the Russian people a deep sense of attachment to the homeland, its fields, settlements and churches. Repeatedly burned by unwelcome aliens Russian villages were restored with heroic persistence and internal humility. And in this desperate persistence and spiritual humility enlightened the loyalty of the Russian man to his culture, historical tradition and the chosen path. A.S.Pushkin poetically expressed it:

"Two senses are remarkably close to us,

There's a heart of food in them:

The love of the native ashes,

Love for my father's coffins.

They've been based on them for centuries.

By the will of God himself.

A man's self-permanent.

The pledge of his greatness.

A life-giving shrine!

The earth would be dead without them.

Without them, our close world is a desert,

The soul is an altar without a deity."

The harsh living conditions gave rise to a propensity to extremes in the Russian people.

"To love, so without reason,

If you threaten, it's not a joke,

To berate, so hot,

If you're gonna rub it in, you're gonna slide it!"

This breadth and extremity in the expression of feelings is not so attractive, if we remember the rampant folk elements in the days of Stepan Razin, Pugachev, peasant unrest and during the civil war A sharp transition from patient obedience to unlimited freedom ended in a heavy bloody hangover.

The cultural self-determination of nations is not something frozen and changes over time. The national character of people changes along with it. But no matter how historical conditions change, no matter how economic, scientific, technical, transport and cultural ties between different peoples are strengthened, each nation is beautiful with its uniqueness, its national language and achievements in literature and art In the world cultural and historical process and in the future, each nation will preserve its uniqueness, expressing the uniqueness of its social experience and destiny.

Mankind, in all its extraordinary diversity, is swept between two cultural poles: East and West. Let's try to clarify these concepts.

It is known that world history began with the East, it is he who is the hearth of civilization. Here the most ancient social and political institutions have emerged and acquired sustainable forms. It's not without reason that the ancient Romans respectfully said, "The light is from the East."

What is East? It is not a geographical concept, but a civilizational, historical and cultural one. It is a gigantic human integrity, very heterogeneous and contradictory.

Eastern culture has some common features: reproduction of established social cultures, stability of the way of life, strict priority of religious and mythological notions and canonized thinking styles, dissolution of personality in the collective.

East is primarily a traditional society and a traditional way of development. Where did this tradition come from, how and by whom was it established? According to orientalists, the tradition was, first of all, borrowed from the cyclical agricultural works, which directly depended on the prosperity of the first centers of civilization. Secondly, having formed themselves in the first state formations, they in every possible way tried to oppose themselves to barbarians and establish their priorities as defining and extremely important.

The main cultural dominance here are myths, religious cults, rituals and rites.

There aren't many civilizations of this kind. Among the civilizations that have been actively functioning nowadays and to a great extent determined the cultural traditions during a number of centuries, we should mention the Arab-Islamic, Indo-Buddhist, Sino-Confucian (Vasiliev L.S. History of the East, 1993, vol. 1, p. 26). Of course, there are many internal differences within each of them, but at the same time, each of them over many centuries of its existence has created a sustainable system of values expressing the specificity of the respective cultural types.

The most important element that characterizes the East' is the 'Eastern Despoty'. Despotism as a form of power and the general structure of society emerges where private property has no priority and land belongs to the rural community. In order to organize intercommunal work, an authority is formed which, gradually gaining strength, becomes despotic towards the community members. However, this authority does not deprive the community of autonomy in solving its own problems. Paying the rent-tax to the state, the community lived with its own concerns, and the community members were not interested in who replaced who at the top of the political pyramid. However, the state governors and their servants were not interested in the joys and troubles of the peasants. The main thing was to get the traditionally established rent-tax on time.

The English historian Toynbee believes that religion is one of the characteristics of civilization and even defines it. Others argue that civilizations choose religion. The Middle East could not accept Christianity with its freedom of conscience and human responsibility for its affairs. But Islam, with its clear regulation of the lives of the faithful, is the best suited to the needs of Middle Eastern civilization.

Differences in worldviews are very significant for the way of life of peoples. Traditional oriental society values various information necessary for organization of everyday life, but it is inhospitable for abstract theoretical studies. As a result, science has been difficult to develop in the East. Neither China nor India has developed modern natural science, although both Chinese and Indians have never been distinguished by mental retardation and have a number of outstanding discoveries and inventions.

It would be an unforgivable misconception to think that the East was standing still. It is true that the dynamics of its development were different from those of the West, albeit slowly. First, its development was cyclical, and the structure rejected those innovations that could threaten its stability. Secondly, in Europe, the engine of progress and supporter of innovation was the citizen-owner. In the East, only those innovations that were in line with corporate ethics and state interests were selected and reproduced. These were innovations aimed at strengthening the effectiveness of power or stability of the state.

In the East, human life is most often adjusted to the rituals of traditional culture without any reverence or indulgence. There is a strict practice of total adaptation of an individual to the rule, rather than rule to an individual. Usually violence against a person in the name of a distracted ideal. The value of human life and its personal uniqueness mean nothing. Personality is replaced by role, i.e., the place of a living person is occupied by a class-based abstract scheme. Within its framework, there is no room for personal will and personal action.

In V.Solovyov's opinion, the Western civilization is directly opposite to the East. "Here we see rapid and continuous development, free play of forces, independence and exceptional self-assertion of all private forms and individual elements" (Solovyev B. C., Works, I. e. 23).

The term "West" refers to a special type of civilized and cultural development that took shape in Europe around the XV-XVII centuries. The predecessors of this type were the culture of antiquity and the Christian tradition. It is in the culture of antiquity that philosophical and religious consciousness loses its monopoly, and a system of quick logical assimilation of knowledge emerges. The forced connection of an individual with tradition collapses, and society loses its unified system of values.

One of the most important factors that influenced the formation of Western civilization was ancient Greek philosophy. Only it formulated an unprecedented for its time idea of love to knowledge in itself. It was not an impersonal Tao or Nirvana, but a logo, which was intelligently understood through the comprehension of nature.

Common historical experience shows that Western European civilization was in crisis, not least because of its narrow culture. "Excessive development of individualism in the modern West leads directly to its opposite - general impersonalization and desecration" (Solovyev B. C., Works, I. e. 25).

The world of mass consumption has completely absorbed and subjugated the European. Possession of things in accordance with advertising, increased density of consumption of various attributes of comfort became his idol. Love replaced sex, friendship replaced money, and care for one's neighbour replaced squeamish handout to a loser. Even in the last century K.D. Kavelin rightly wrote: "Western Europeans have forgotten the inner, moral, spiritual world of a man to whom the gospel sermon is addressed. The latter is, as it seems to me, the Achilles' heel of European civilization; here are the roots of the disease that sharpens and digs up its powers. The Western European gave himself to the development of objective conditions of existence in the belief that they alone hide the mystery of human well-being and perfection: the subjective side in complete disregard" (Kavelin K.D. Our mental system, M., 1989. p. 465).

Analyzing the Western civilization, V. Solovyov noted that in the field of knowledge, it suffered the same fate as in public life. Christian zeal to understand the meaning of life was replaced by increased technological subjugation of natural forces for practical benefit. The consequence of this was the loss of a unifying spiritual element in society. Western civilization thus condemns people to petty practicality and care for the bank account. Although it is fashionable to talk about individual rights, rights themselves are understood in a very limited way. Emphasis is placed not on the individual, but on his selfishness and individualism, on his right to sacrifice his family, his state, his ethnos, and his homeland to his benefit.

Expressing a deep difference between Eastern and Western civilizations, the famous English writer R. Kipling said: "East is East, and West is West, and they will never get together". These words do not contain all the truth. The modern crisis of industrial society, its orientation to technological, economic and political rationalism, mass production and consumption make it necessary to pay attention to the values of traditional Eastern society, to the achievements of Chinese, Indian, Arab and Iranian-Islamic culture. Without a dialogue between East and West, humanity has no future.

It is well known that traditional principles play a huge role in Russian civilization. Sobornost, collectivity, serving its people, i.e. the priority of national interests over personal concerns, antipragmatic mood - all these are essential features of Russian culture. The culture of the Russian nation was formed in many ways as an acute humanistic reaction to the disorganization and administrative arbitrariness in practical life, which burdened our ancestors.

Russian culture has always had a strange "compensatory" mechanism of development, the essence of which is a self-forgetful quest for pure ideals and a response to external violence.

Indeed, the worse things were going on in the country, the more zealously the Russian soul rushed into the realm of good, justice and truth. The result of this impulse is an imaginary hailstorm Kitezh, fanaticism Avvakum, the image of "Holy Russia", sectarianism, going to the people, the Russian idea. The fact that it was in Russia of the XIX century, "suffering from the barbaric remnants of serfdom, inferior to its European neighbors on many parameters of economic and political improvement, an unprecedented rise in art, were created timeless masterpieces that conquered the "fed and tranquil" Europe. Similarly, brilliant successes of the "Silver Age" were achieved by Russia in the conditions of a dying empire, on the eve of the coming social transformation of the country.

All listed principles are peculiar to Russian people and are vital in conditions of a severe climate and not less severe history. "All our activity and forces have been absorbed exclusively by development of one direct external conditions of state and national existence. Centuries have passed in these concerns, in the struggle for existence, in the development of the first rudiments of citizenship and language" (K.D. Kavelin, Our mental system, M., 1989, p. 281).

Kavalin's thought cannot be understood in the sense that for centuries the Russian people have been engaged only in that struggle for the external conditionality of their existence, forgetting about spiritual food. On the contrary, the Russian people stood up against numerous opponents only because they had a high culture. Neither the East in the face of Islamized nomads, nor the West in the face of Catholicized robbers-knights could offer the Russian people} higher spiritual values than those which they themselves had developed on the basis of Orthodoxy accepted by them.

The peculiarity of each culture is most fully revealed in the so-called critical periods of its history. For Russia, this period was Peter the Great's reforms. Peter turned his face to the West. Technical and scientific achievements of Western European countries delighted him. Common sense told him that it was impossible to develop the country, literacy and health care without abrupt socio-cultural transformations.

Peter and his entourage had ignited the country's passions and contributed to the formation of spiritual opposition to his reforms. Dialogue of Russian culture with European culture or Europeanization of Russian culture? If the Europeanization of Russian culture, then blind borrowing or critical attitude to the West? Such an acute question arose in the 18th century for Russia.

Petrovsky's reforms shook Russia up, leaving no one indifferent in evaluating the results achieved and determining further ways of the country's development. One of the consequences of deep reflections on the fate of his homeland was the formation of Westernism, Slavophilism, and then Eurasianism among the Russian intelligentsia.

Westerners (P.Y.Chaadayev, N.V.Stankevich, V.G.Belinsky, A.I.Herzen) connected the future of the country with the assimilation and adaptation of historical achievements of Western Europe.

Of course, Russia could not stay within the framework of traditional civilization forever, and sooner or later it had to embark on the path of building an industrial society. The Western European countries were an example in this respect. The development of science and technology in the West made progress, thus ensuring the scientific and technological superiority of the West over the East.

For Russia, the successes of the West in education, health care, democracy and everyday life have been contagious. Already in the XVII century, the achievements of everyday life and technology, and then Western European ideas began to penetrate into Moscow. Russia's acquaintance with Western European culture was inevitable. The Westerners were in favor of this acquisition.

Slavophiles (I.V.Kireevsky, A.S.Khomyakov, K.S.Aksakov, Y.F.Samarin) spoke out against Europeanization, but the dialogue with the West. They proposed the doctrine of sobornost, autocracy and Orthodoxy. These three principles, in opinion of Slavophiles, define the structure of Russia, way of life of the Russian population and its morality. Slavophiles categorically opposed blind assimilation by the country of forms of the Western European political life. Excessive rationalization of culture of the West, its bourgeois practicalism and utilitarianism, considered Slavophiles, kills spirituality, transforms the person in calculating egoist.

In their polemics with Westerners, Slavophiles were not tired of reminding about the crusades organized by Catholics to the Russian land, about the outrageous behavior of the Polish gentry in Moscow during the Time of

Troubles, and about the way of life of Peter the Great's time workers, which was defiant to Russian culture. "All the appearance of European culture was assimilated without any changes, completely mechanically... And sweet food, and soft beds, and elegant idleness of the highest class, and the luxury of the environment, costume, housing - all this became commonplace" (Milyukov P.N., Essays on the history of Russian culture, 1993. vol. 3. p. 131).

Unfortunately, criticism of Europeanization of Russian culture among Slavophiles was often accompanied by idealization of traditional, patriarchal relations in the country, protection of autocracy and ritual religiosity. Meanwhile, the country needed changes, spreading education, building schools and scientific institutions, and democratizing public life.

Naturally, it is necessary to refer to the world experience in reforming social and economic orders. Here too, the originality of culture cannot be considered as a ban on its enrichment with the cultural achievements of other nations.

In 1921, there was also a third point of view - Eurasianism - about Russia's place in the dialogue between West and East. Its representatives are N.S.Trubetskoy, P.N.Savitsky, G.V.Vernadsky, L.N.Gumilev. The original feature of Eurasianism is the emphasis on Asia, the Asian component of Russia. The West is skeptical about Russia's claim to be a European power. Its politicians believe that Russia in Europe is some foreign body. They are particularly dislikeful of Orthodoxy.

In his work "Europe and Mankind" N. Trubetskoy wrote that the orientation of Eastern European peoples to the West is detrimental to their original culture. Especially dangerous for their future" is the opinion spread by Western European politicians about their inferiority. Conceding to this opinion entails a separation from one's own history, a forgetfulness of cultural traditions.

"The hidden dream of every European is the impersonalization of all the peoples of the globe, the destruction of all the original forms of cultures, except one European ... who wants to be known as universal, and all other cultures to turn into second class cultures" (Gumilev LN Rhythms of Eurasia, M., 1993. P. 54). Developing an idea that each ethnos is most closely connected with a landscape, a place of development, L.N.Gumilev concludes that the universal culture, identical for all peoples, is impossible. There cannot be a single cultural center on the globe. Variety of natural conditions requires polycentrism.

Russia is a unique country with a unique culture that is adequate to both geographical conditions and its historical traditions and the national character of the Russian nation. And neither European nationalism nor cosmopolitanism is acceptable to it. Back at the end of the last century Kavelin noted in a letter to Dostoevsky that the main mistake of Westerners was that they looked at European ideas as universal. In fact, they were the birth of European nationalism and industrial society. Russia needs the achievements of the European civilization, but not in order for Russians to become Europeans and lose their identity, but in order to take into account the achievements of world science and technology, to choose from world culture that corresponds to its traditions and strengthens its identity. Russia is close and understandable to J. Nehru's words that "it was Asia that gave great ideological leaders, who may have had more influence on the world than anyone else or anything else anywhere. Asia has given great founders of major religions" (Nehru J. Look at World History, 2004. vol. 1. p. 41). V.S.Solovyov sharply spoke about that part of Russian intelligentsia which "instead of the image and likeness of God still continues to carry the image and likeness of an ape" and called before the West "to restore in itself the Russian folk character, to stop creating an idol for itself from any narrow insignificant idea ...". to become more indifferent to the limited interests of this life, to believe freely and reasonably in another, higher reality" (Solovyev B. C. Works, vol. 1, p. 31).

The culture of both the West and the East is full of timeless spiritual values. Nowadays, the process of integration and mutual enrichment of cultures is unstoppable. With its advantageous geographical location, taking into account its Eurasianism and based on the richness of its culture, Russia is able to promote dialogue between West and East and make its own contribution to this dialogue.

By participating in the dialogue between East and West, Russia will preserve its identity and independence, its Orthodox face and its collectivist principles. Only then will it be lucky to become an exemplary state both in political and economic, scientific and technological, and cultural and moral respects.

Russian culture is a historical and multifaceted concept. It includes facts, processes, trends that testify to long and complex development both in geographical space and in historical time. The remarkable representative of the European Renaissance, Maxim Greeks, who moved to our country at the turn of the 16th century, has an amazing image of Russia in terms of depth and loyalty. He writes about her as a woman in a black dress, thoughtfully sitting "on the road". Russian culture is also "on the road", it is formed and developed in constant search. This is evidenced by...

history.

Most of Russia's territory is inhabited later than those regions of the world where the main centers of world culture have formed. In this sense, Russian culture is a relatively young phenomenon. Moreover, Russia did not know the period of slavery: the Eastern Slavs passed directly to feudalism from community-patriarchal relations. Due to its historical youth, Russian culture was faced with the need for intensive historical development. Of course, Russian culture developed under the influence of different cultures of the countries of the West and East, which historically preceded Russia. But perceiving and assimilating the cultural heritage of other peoples, Russian writers and artists, sculptors and architects, scientists and philosophers solved their problems, formed and developed the domestic traditions, never limiting themselves to copying other people's samples.

The long period of development of Russian culture was determined by the Chryso-Tian Orthodox religion. For many centuries the leading cultural genres were temple construction, icon painting, church literature. Russia, up to the XVIII century, made a significant contribution to the world art treasury with its spiritual activities related to Christianity.

At the same time, the impact of Christianity on Russian culture is far from being unequivocal. According to a fair comment of a prominent Slavophile A. S. Khomyakov, Russia has accepted only the external form, ritual, and not the spirit and essence of the Christian religion. Russian culture has left under influence of religious dogmata and has outgrown borders of Orthodoxy.

The specific features of Russian culture are largely determined by what researchers have called the "character of the Russian people". All researchers of "Russian idea" wrote about it. The main feature of this character was called faith. The alternative "faith-knowledge", "faith-smart" was decided in Russia in specific historical periods in different ways, but most often in favor of faith. Russian culture testifies: for all the differences in the Russian soul and Russian character it is difficult to disagree with the famous lines of F. Tyutchev: "Russia cannot be understood by the mind, it is impossible to measure a common arson: it has a special become - one can only believe in Russia".

Russian culture has accumulated great values. The task of present generations is to preserve and multiply them.

# Used literature


1.	Buganov V.I., Ziryanov P.N. History of Russia, Moscow, "Enlightenment", 2007.

2.	Vasiliev L.S. History of the East, 1993, vol.1.

3.	Greeks I.B., Chessmagonov F.F. World of History. Russian lands in XIII-XV centuries. Moscow: The Guard, 1986.

4.	Gumilev L.N. Rhythms of Eurasia, Moscow, 1993.

5.	Danilov A.A., Kosulina L.G. History of Russia, Moscow, "Enlightenment", 2006.

6.	Dmitrenko V.P., Esakov V.D., Shestakov V.A. History of Fatherland, "Drofa", 2005.

7.	Zuev M.N. History of Russia, M., "Drofa", 2004.

8.	Izbornik: Stories of Ancient Russia / Composition. and examples. L. Dmitrieva and N. Ponyrko; Will enter, article D. Likhachev. M., Khudozhka. lit., 1986.

9.	History of the Fatherland. (Short course, issue 1-2), Moscow, 1992, "Znanie" society of Russian Federation, author's collective.

10.	History of Russia. Under edition of A.A. Radugin, Publishing house "Center", Moscow, 2001.

11.	Cavelyn K.D. Our mental system, M., 1989.

12.	Katsva L.A., Yurganov A.L. History of Russia, Moscow, MIros - ARGOS, Moscow, 2005.

13.	Leontyeva G.A., Shorin P.A., Kobrin V.B. luchies to the secrets of Clio. M., "Enlightenment", 1994.

14.	Lossky I.O. Conditions of absolute good. M., 1991

15.	Milyukov P.N., Essays on the History of Russian Culture, 1993. t. 3

16.	Nehru J. Look at World History. M., 2004. t. 1.

17.	Stories of Russian chronicles of XV-XVII centuries. Per. with Ancient Russians. Composition, foreword, per. and explanations by T.N. Mikhelson. Ed. by D.S. Likhachev, M., "Det. lit.", 1976.

18.	Solovyev B. C. Essays, t. 1.

19.	Philosophy. Edited by A.G. M. Spirkin, 1999.

20.	Chivilikhin V."A. Memory: A novel essay. M., Artist. lit. 1984

Printed by Books on Demand GmbH, Norderstedt / Germany